CONTENTS

John Dean became a household name during the Watergate scandal of the early 1970's. Of the thirty-five "President's men" listed in Bernstein and Woodward's classic exposé, *All the President's Men*, Dean had one of the most significant roles in ending the cover-up.

Richard Nixon's presidency began to unravel on June 17, 1972, when members of the Committee to Re-elect the President were caught trying to bug Democratic headquarters at the Watergate. The ensuing cover-up destroyed the President's credibility and led to his resignation on August 8, 1974.

Along the way, numerous Nixon staff members were implicated in the cover-up and convicted of various offenses. Chuck Colson, G. Gordon Liddy, John D. Ehrlichman, and H. R. Haldeman each became well known for their involvement.

John Dean took a particularly prominent position in the Watergate proceedings. As White House Counsel under Richard Nixon, Dean was privy to secret information that implicated the President and others in the famous break-in and subsequent cover-up. He became the star witness of the Watergate investigation, and will long be remembered for his role in uncovering the scandal.

In his fascinating historical work, *Watergate: The Corruption of American Politics and the Fall of Richard Nixon*, Fred Emery explains that:

> In return for limiting his conviction to a single felony of conspiracy to obstruct justice, Dean would pledge his complete cooperation with the prosecution,...[1]

Dean's cooperation proved invaluable to the prosecution. But, Emery explains, he was ultimately sentenced to a minimum of one year in jail.[2]

Despite his conviction, Dean is considered by many to have behaved honorably by seeking to end the cover-up and by testifying honestly, even though doing so meant personal embarrassment and the conviction of many of his former associates. Regardless of one's view of Dean, he undoubtedly played a historically significant role in the Watergate proceedings.

---

[1] Fred Emery, *Watergate: The Corruption of American Politics and the Fall of Richard Nixon* (1994), 393.

[2] *Id.*, at 463.

Dean is by all accounts an intelligent, articulate man. Prior to his involvement in the Nixon administration, he earned a law degree from Georgetown University and served in the office of the U.S. Attorney General. He has written a number of books, including several related to Watergate.

His latest book, published in July 2006, is entitled *Conservatives Without Conscience.* As an individual who knew and worked with many of the most powerful conservatives of the early 1970's, Dean might be expected to offer an interesting perspective on today's conservative movement. The cover of the book features pictures of Lewis Libby, Tom Delay, Jack Abramoff, Dick Cheney, Karl Rove, Bill Frist, and Pat Robertson – seven of the most powerful and conservative men of the day.

Dean's book shot to the top tier of bestseller lists upon its release. Many newspapers and pundits praised the book for offering fresh insights into the conservative movement.

Like many readers, I expected the book to contain a thorough, well-supported, and logically coherent analysis of today's conservative movement. And, like many, I was disappointed.

Conservatives Without Conscience argues that today's conservative movement has become authoritarian. Dean sees this as a bad trend and does not hesitate to identify specific alleged authoritarians by name. In support of his claims, he cites psychological research conducted by Bob Altemeyer, a Canadian professor.

The purpose of this book is not to attack the facts presented in Dean's book. I assume, for the sake of this argument, that all of his facts are correct. There may be factual errors in Dean's book, but an analysis of such errors would be beyond the scope of this work.

The purpose of this book is to identify logical errors in Dean's argument. And there are plenty. Undoubtedly, some of Dean's inconsistencies have escaped my notice. The errors I *have* noticed, however, seriously undermine Dean's conclusions.

I realize that to committed anti-conservatives, Dean's logical errors will not matter. Those who dislike today's conservatives can cheer to Dean's rhetoric, whether they find it logically coherent or not. Such people are what I call "Liberals Without Logic."

For the objective, open-minded reader, however, Dean's logical errors *do* matter.

Political discourse today is tainted by mudslinging and name-calling. In the realm of political discussion, what is needed most is unbiased discussion – arguments based on reliable, scientific evidence.

To achieve this type of objective discourse, we must be willing to refute unsupported arguments when they are made. I believe, therefore, that the critique contained in this book is a necessary contribution to the current debate about conservatism in America.

PART I: CREDIBILITY

CHAPTER 1

DEFINITION OF A CONSERVATIVE

Conservatives Without Conscience, the latest book by John W. Dean, is, not surprisingly, a book about conservatives. One would expect such a book to define the term "conservative" precisely. Without a precise definition, the reader would not know who was being accused of lacking a conscience. Besides, there is no point in writing two hundred pages of criticism about a group unless that group is clearly identified.

If, as the title of Dean's book suggests, these conservatives lack consciences, the public needs to know who they are. Lacking a conscience is, presumably, a bad thing. It might even be dangerous. Surely, *Conservatives Without Conscience* would identify these conservatives carefully.

Surprisingly, Dean's book does not offer a precise definition of "conservative." To the contrary, the subheading at the top of page 2 states: "Conservatism Cannot Be Meaningfully Defined." This subheading is followed by thirty pages of text, explaining why "conservative" is such a slippery term. The text introduces various definitions of the term "conservative." Nowhere, however, does it tell the reader what John Dean means when he uses the word.

Dean's failure to define "conservative" renders many of his allegations nonsensical. For example, on page 12, he states that "nothing in America's founding, or the creation of the United States, was of a conservative nature." How could he possibly know that, if he does not know what the word "conservative" means? Or, for that matter, how could he know *anything* about conservatives without having a clear idea of who they are? *Conservatives Without Conscience* uses the term "conservative" constantly, but none of its statements has a clear meaning because the word "conservative" is not given a clear meaning.

More significantly, by not defining "conservative," Dean prevents readers from evaluating the truth of his arguments. If Dean states that conservatives act a certain way, it is difficult to disagree with him unless one first discovers what he means by "conservative." As long as that term is vague and undefined, it is impossible to disprove any of the author's allegations.

For example, on page 26, Dean writes that, conservatives "have little facility for self-analysis." An observant reader might point out that Bob Dole, a conservative, recently wrote a three-hundred-page memoir. Surely that undertaking required more than a little facility for self-analysis. A defender of Dean's allegations, however, can counter that Bob Dole is not a conservative. It would be impossible to disagree with that defense, because Dean never settles on a definition of "conservative."

All we really know about Dean's modern "conservatives" is that he does not entirely approve of them. And that might tell us as much about him as it does about them.

CHAPTER 2

A WORKING DEFINITION

The first thirty pages of Dean's book offer numerous definitions of "conservative," none of which meet with Dean's unequivocal approval. Along the way, he introduces and refutes the argument that conservatives have no true ideology. He, evidently, does believe that conservatism is a true ideology. Unfortunately, he does not clearly define it.

Dean also argues that there are no conservative leaders sufficiently authoritative to settle the issue. That is an interesting admission, because the remainder of the book attempts to show that conservatives are extremely authoritarian, meaning that conservatives tend to fall in line behind their leaders. If they are so easily led, why is there no authoritative conservative leader to define the term "conservative?" Dean does not say.

For purposes of this work, we need a definition of "conservative." As noted above, Dean's arguments cannot be checked for logical consistency if critical terms like "conservative" are left undefined. It is important, however, that we settle on a definition that is basically consistent with Dean's thinking.

The definition of "conservative" that seems to receive the most approval from Dean is the Janda-Berry-Goldman definition presented on pages thirty-five through thirty-seven of *Conservatives Without Conscience*. Under this definition, a conservative is someone who opposes "government activities that interfere with the market" and favors "government actions that impose social order."[3]

A person who opposes government activities that interfere with the market might oppose the following measures: tax increases, regulation of businesses, price controls, minimum wages laws, and so forth.

A person who favors government actions that impose social order might support government restrictions on: abortion, homosexual marriage, illegal drugs, and so forth.

---

[3] John W. Dean, CONSERVATIVES WITHOUT CONSCIENCE (2006), pages 35-37, citing Kenneth Janda and Jeffrey M. Berry, THE CHALLENGE OF DEMOCRACY: GOVERNMENT IN AMERICA (Dean does not identify the relevant edition).

For purposes of this work, we will use the Janda-Berry-Goldman definition of "conservative." It is attractive because of its simplicity. Additionally, it seems to fairly portray common views about what it means to be a conservative.

Application of the Definition

Armed with this definition, we can perform a meaningful analysis of Dean's book. For example, as noted above, page 26 of *Conservatives Without Conscience* states that conservatives "have little facility for self-analysis." We know that Bob Dole is a conservative, because he opposes government activities that interfere with the market (e.g., by promoting welfare reform) and favors government actions that impose social order (e.g., by supporting the war on drugs). But Bob Dole has demonstrated a significant facility for self-analysis by writing a three-hundred-page memoir. The statement on page 26 of Dean's book, therefore, does not correctly describe all conservatives.

Over the course of this work, we will find that many of the arguments contained in *Conservatives Without Conscience* fall apart when examined closely. By insisting on precise definitions of terms used in Dean's book, we can fairly examine its arguments.

It is important to note, however, that the fact that Dean fails to support an allegation does not necessarily mean that the allegation is false. For example, when Dean states that "about 20 to 25 percent of the adult American population is so right-wing authoritarian,… [that they] would march America into a dictatorship and probably feel that things had improved as a result,"[4] his argument fails for lack of evidence. It may, in fact, be true that 20 to 25 percent of Americans would feel good about marching America into a dictatorship, but Dean has not proven it to be true.

This work merely identifies the logical failures in *Conservatives Without Conscience*. It does not propose counterarguments. Nor does it make claims about the truth or falsehood of Dean's contentions.

---

[4] John W. Dean, CONSERVATIVES WITHOUT CONSCIENCE (2006), page 184.

CHAPTER 3

THE IMPORTANCE OF BEING CONSERVATIVE

John Dean had tremendous credibility as a witness in the Watergate investigation. He had served within the Nixon administration, and had solid conservative credentials. As a member of the President's staff, he was presumed to be loyal to the President and other top conservative leaders. It would not be reasonable to expect him to testify falsely against conservatives, because they were his friends, colleagues and fellow ideologues. If anything, a man in his position could be expected to color the truth in order to protect other conservatives.

When, in the course of the investigation, he spoke out against fellow conservatives, therefore, people took him seriously. To many, he was seen as a principled conservative. Rather than lie to protect his comrades, he would expose the truth. One could not help but feel, however, that the potential damage to the conservative movement was personally painful to him.

Dean attempts to establish a similar level of credibility in *Conservatives Without Conscience*. He begins the book by explaining his history with the conservative movement at length. If he can establish himself as a true conservative speaking out against the wrongdoing of other conservatives, he will once again be afforded a high degree of credibility. After all, why would a loyal conservative make accusations against other conservatives if they were not true? Readers will naturally conclude that something must be seriously wrong with the conservative movement if one of its own prominent members has begun criticizing it. And there is no question that Dean's book does criticize the modern conservative movement.

But if Dean is not a conservative, he does not have much credibility. A non-conservative could have any number of reasons to claim that modern conservatives lack conscience. A liberal (or a libertarian, socialist, or any other brand of ideologue) might want to vilify conservatives so that his own ideology looks more attractive by comparison. Alternatively, a liberal might have an axe to grind with certain conservative rivals. A public figure who is not loyal to the modern conservative movement might write a book attacking conservatives for financial reasons; in the current political climate, books critical of conservatisms seem to find their way onto the bestseller lists quite easily.

In short, the persuasive power of *Conservatives Without Conscience* rests, in large measure, on the issue of whether John Dean is a conservative. He calls himself a conservative, but a truly critical reader cannot take the author's word at face value. *Conservatives Without Conscience* warns of the dangers of being uncritical toward authorities.[5] We must oblige, therefore, and be critical of Dean's own statements. We must evaluate for ourselves whether Dean is truly conservative.

---

[5] *See, e.g.,* John W. Dean, CONSERVATIVES WITHOUT CONSCIENCE (2006), page 69.

CHAPTER 4

THE CONSERVATIVE TEST

To determine whether John Dean is a conservative, we turn to the Janda-Berry-Goldman definition, which he provided. As the reader will recall, this definition posits that a conservative is someone who opposes "government activities that interfere with the market" and favors "government actions that impose social order."

If Dean's political views fall within the Janda-Berry-Goldman definition, then he is a conservative for purposes of our analysis. If his views do not fall within the definition, then he is not a conservative. It is not necessary to decide whether he is a liberal or some other type of ideologue. For the purpose of evaluating Dean's credibility, we need only decide whether he is a conservative or not.

To apply the Janda-Berry-Goldman definition, we must determine what Dean's political views are. To do so, we will rely on the text of *Conservatives Without Conscience*. We will not attempt to analyze Mr. Dean's public acts, his other writings, or his reputation. Those sources of information are beyond the scope of this work. Additionally, there is a danger that we might be selective in pulling information from such a wide collection of sources. Instead, we will focus only on the admissions contained in his recent book.

Question 1: Does Dean oppose government activities that interfere with the market?

Dean does not explicitly state whether he opposes government activities that interfere with the market. In his entire book, however, Dean never criticizes a conservative for opposing government activities that interfere with the market. Dean criticizes them for various other perceived faults, but not for this one. This suggests that Dean does not see anything wrong with opposing government activities that interfere with the market. It seems likely, therefore, that he himself opposes government activities that interfere with the market.

Question 2: Does Dean favor government actions that impose social order?

Conservatives Without Conscience is highly critical of conservative efforts to impose social order. Dean accuses Christian conservatives of pushing such measures as limitations on abortion, banning of gay marriage, opposition to sex education, opposition to stem cell research, and so forth.[6] Much of the book is dedicated to criticism of various forms of social legislation. It is likely, therefore, that Dean does not favor government actions that impose social order.

This analysis is not extremely reliable, because Dean says little about his own political views in the course of his work. Based on the limited information available, however, it appears that Dean passes the first prong of the conservative test, but fails the second prong. According to the Janda-Berry-Goldman chart reproduced on page 37 of Dean's book, Dean could be classified as a libertarian. Further support for that conclusion is found in the fact that Dean cites the Cato Institute and other libertarian thinkers several times in his book. For our purposes, however, the relevant fact is that Dean does not appear to be a true conservative.

The conclusion that Dean is not a conservative is consistent with statements in his book. Dean opines at one point that, "the Grand Old Party to which I once

---

[6] *See, e.g., Id.,* at 108-9.

belonged has moved so far to the right, that on the contemporary political spectrum I now often fall to the left of the Republican center."[7] We learn from this statement that Dean does not consider himself a Republican, and that he believes the party is more conservative than he is. Elsewhere, he states that the Brookings Institution was "once liberal (now moderate),"[8] and that "there is not a single true liberal on the high Court [i.e., the U.S. Supreme Court]."[9] Conventional wisdom holds that Brookings is liberal and that three, possibly four, of the Supreme Court Justices are true liberals. Nevertheless, Dean believes these important institutions have shifted right (i.e., toward political conservatism).

If American's political institution have shifted right, relative to Dean, there are three possible explanations: (1) Dean's ideology has remained unchanged while everyone else has become more conservative, (2) Dean's ideology has changed (becoming less conservative) while everyone else has remained unchanged, or (3) Dean's ideology has changed and everyone else has become more conservative. Option number one appears unlikely. In politics, change is the rule for individuals as well as for parties and institutions.

---

[7] *Id.*, at xxxiii.
[8] *Id.*, at 91.
[9] *Id.*, at 109.

Dean is far enough to the left of today's political institutions to write a book harshly criticizing dozens of conservative leaders on the basis of their beliefs. In the 1960's, Dean may have appropriately labeled himself a conservative. We do not have any evidence to evaluate his ideology at that time. In the present, however, the evidence he provides tends to identify him as a non-conservative.

CHAPTER 5

THE GOLDWATER CONNECTION

To bolster his conservative credentials, Dean relies on Barry M. Goldwater, former U.S. senator and presidential candidate. As Dean notes, Goldwater wrote the classic conservative work, *Conscience of a Conservative*.[10] When he ran for president, Goldwater embodied, for many, the true definition of a conservative.

According to Dean, he and Goldwater planned to write a book about social conservatives entitled *Conservatives Without Conscience*,[11]a play on words referring to Goldwater's earlier book. The former presidential candidate died in 1998, before he and Dean could commence work on the proposed book.

Even if we assume that Goldwater meets our definition of "conservative," Dean's book does not

---

[10] *Id.*, at xxxii.
[11] *Id.*, at xxxv.

necessarily reflect Mr. Goldwater's views. The famous conservative died eight years before the release of *Conservatives Without Conscience*. Dean acknowledges, in fact, that he has "not taken the liberty of attempting to speak for [Goldwater]."[12]

Even if Dean and Goldwater were close friends, that association does not automatically render Dean a conservative. Nor does it confer Goldwater's stamp of approval on Dean's book. Although Goldwater was a famous and important conservative, his connection to Dean does not establish Dean as a conservative.

What Would a Conservative Do?

After reading *Conservatives Without Conscience*, it is difficult to see John Dean as a moderate conservative out to save the conservative movement from extremists. He simply does not write the things a conservative would write under such circumstances.

A true conservative mourning the state of conservatism would offer solutions. He would suggest that conservatives should hold their own accountable for bad acts. Maybe he would suggest that conservative candidates stop mudslinging or dedicate themselves to teaching young conservatives to be civil and have a sense of honor. But John Dean does none of that.

---

[12] *Id.*, at xxxvi.

A true conservative would address his remarks to other conservatives. Dean does not do that. Instead, he opens the chapters of his book with statements such as the following:

> Answers to questions such as why so many conservatives are hostile and mean-spirited, why they embrace false history, and why they take on a cause like attempting to impeach President Clinton despite public opposition to the undertaking are not found in any traditional conservative philosophy – however that attitude might be defined or described.[13]

If John Dean is trying to appeal to conservatives with his new book, he does not understand his audience. Statements like the one quoted above are not likely to appeal to even the most jaded of modern conservatives. But John Dean has an extensive history with the conservative movement, and he is undoubtedly aware of how statements like the above will be taken by most conservatives. It is reasonable to conclude, therefore, that such statements are not intended for a conservative audience.

Conservatives Without Conscience is written for a non-conservative audience. It does not ask conservatives to behave differently. Instead, it warns non-conservatives of the dangers posed by modern conservatives.

____

[13] *Id.*, at 39.

In short, John Dean has not written a book about "us." He has written a book about "them."

Because Dean is not a modern conservative, his criticisms lack credibility. An objective reader should, therefore, be skeptical of his claims.

PART II: RATIONALITY

CHAPTER 6

LOGIC

Even if Dean does not have strong conservative credentials, his arguments might still be correct. If they have adequate factual support and are logically consistent, then Dean's lack of credibility will not render them false. Like any political group, conservatives may be the subject of legitimate criticism. If legitimate issues are raised in Dean's book and defended rationally, then objective readers will be forced to accept them as true, no matter how negatively they reflect on conservatives.

One would expect Dean to adhere closely to rules of logic because throughout *Conservatives Without Conscience* he complains about the irrationality of certain conservatives. Surely, then, he must be strictly rational in his own arguments.

Dean suggests, however, that rationality is not always necessary. In a passage about torture, he cites Professor

David Luban and philosopher Bernard Williams for the idea that, "there are certain situations so monstrous that the idea that the processes of moral rationality could yield an answer in them is insane..."[14] Unfortunately, Dean does not analyze this statement. He merely produces it to show that no response is necessary to a particular conservative argument.

Dean does not explain what would make a situation so monstrous that the application of moral rationality becomes insane. If, for example, one felt that conservative authoritarians were threatening the future of a country, would one be justified in abandoning rationality in one's arguments? If so, why? It seems that logical reasoning would always be an acceptable method of supporting one's position. Failure to use logic in one's defense might imply that one *has* no logical defense. Surely its best to make logical arguments in one's defense if such arguments exist.

Dean also fails to explain what method of discovering truth should be used in place of rationality in one of these monstrous situations. Should people turn to some sort of mysticism to find the truth? Dean's book is quite critical of Christian conservatives, so it seems unlikely that he would advocate turning to the Bible for answers. Should people simply trust their leaders? That idea

---

[14] *Id.*, at 165.

seems inconsistent with Dean's book, as well. In a monstrous situation, should people simply accept Dean's conclusions without demanding logical support?

It is surprising that an author would suggest abandoning rationality for any reason. What is Dean's book, if not a series of purportedly logical arguments? If reason is not required, then there is no point in debating political issues.

The arguments of *Conservatives Without Conscience* do, in fact, demonstrate a lack of logical consistency and factual evidence. These shortcomings undermine Dean's arguments. Consider, for example, the following argument Dean makes about conservatives:

Conservatives are Irrational

One of Dean's fundamental tenets is that conservatives are irrational. Page 27 of *Conservatives Without Conscience* begins with the heading: "Conservatives Are Often Illogical, Inconsistent, and Contradictory." "Social conservatives," explains Dean, "are especially susceptible to irrational beliefs,..." He does not cite Luban and Williams in these conservatives' defense. These conservatives, apparently, do not find themselves in situations sufficiently monstrous to suspend the requirements of rationality.

It is difficult to believe that conservatives are more susceptible to irrational beliefs than any other group of people. In a serious work of social science, a sweeping generalization like the one Dean makes here would require extensive statistical support. Surveys of adequate sample sizes would be needed to establish the level of irrationality among non-conservatives and the level of irrationality among conservatives. The two groups could then be compared, and one could judge (1) whether conservatives truly are susceptible to irrational beliefs and (2) whether that fact makes them different from the population at large.

Dean does not, however, feel a need to support his generalizations with statistical data. For Dean, two anecdotes and a scripture will suffice:

> **Anecdote 1**: According to Dean, certain conservatives support their opposition to abortion by saying they believe in a "culture of life," even though they simultaneously support the death penalty. Dean says the hypocritical conservatives explain away this inconsistency by saying that "[t]he unborn are innocent while those being executed are not,..."[15] That seems like a reasonable distinction, but Dean finds it irrational.

---

[15] *Id.*, at 27.

Anecdote 2: Dean then explains that conservatives oppose efforts to alter the Pledge of Allegiance by removing the phrase "under God," and by doing so deny the Pledge's "liberty and justice for all" to atheists who don't want the Pledge to say "under God." Although this behavior seems irrational to Dean, its possible that conservatives simply disagree with him about what liberty and justice require. At any rate, insisting on the phrase "under God" might be rational behavior for someone with conservative religious values.

Scripture: Finally, Dean claims that conservatives are hypocritical because they want to have prayer in public schools even though the Bible states, in Matthew 6:5-7: *"But when you pray, go into your room, close the door and pray* to your Father, who is unseen."[16] Dean interprets this scripture to mean that prayer should be confined to private spaces. This seems like a minor criticism, because reasonable minds can disagree over the proper application of scripture.

Elsewhere in his book, Dean cites Jimmy Carter for the maxim that "Bible quoting in politics is

---

[16] *Id.*, at 27 (the emphasis is Dean's).

fruitless."[17] In this case, at least, he makes an exception for himself.

Dean's two anecdotes and a scripture do not necessarily demonstrate irrationality on the part of conservatives. In each case, it is possible to discover a rational explanation for the behavior of the conservatives. This "evidence" merely shows that Dean disagrees with conservatives on some issues.

Even if each of Dean's two anecdotes and a scripture clearly demonstrated conservative irrationality, they would not be sufficient to support his claim that "social conservatives are especially susceptible to irrational beliefs." The word "especially" implies that conservatives are more susceptible to irrational beliefs than other groups are. With little effort, however, one could find three examples of irrationality on the part of almost any group of people. Political groups are easy targets, because they take so many policy positions. Inevitably, some of the positions taken will conflict with one another. In this regard, conservatives (social or otherwise) are not unique. Dean presents no evidence that conservatives are "especially" susceptible to irrational beliefs.

---

[17] *Id.*, at 101.

For liberals without logic, however, Dean's evidence will suffice. A dedicated anti-conservative does not need strong evidence that conservatives are irrational. To the hardcore liberal, the fact is self-evident. All that is needed, therefore, is the color of reasoning – a few arguments that sound like factual support. And that's what Dean provides.

CHAPTER 7

MORE ABOUT CONSERVATIVES

Not only are conservatives irrational, Dean argues, but they also react poorly when you try to tell them how irrational they are! *Conservatives Without Conscience* explains that, "If made cognizant of [their illogical thinking], they [the Conservatives] either rationalize it away, neglect to care, or attack those who reveal their human weaknesses."[18]

Stated in more neutral terms, conservatives who are accused of irrationality react by:

1. Rejecting the idea that they are irrational;
2. Doing nothing; or
3. Actively opposing their accusers.

____

[18] *Id.*, at 27.

These are the basic responses one would expect from anyone accused of irrationality. They are simply defensive reactions to criticism.

Humans of all stripes react defensively when accused of irrationality or any other bad trait. When liberals (or any other type of ideologues) are accused of irrationality, they probably reject the accusation, do nothing, or oppose their accusers, just as conservatives do. Dean does not comment on the reactions of other political groups, though. He presents no evidence that conservatives are more defensive than others. In fact, he presents no evidence of their defensive behaviors at all.

Presumably, Dean would like conservatives to respond to accusations of irrationality by admitting their irrationality and then changing their beliefs to align with Dean's. But it is not surprising that conservatives rarely react in that way.

In a bizarre passage near the end of *Conservatives Without Conscience*, Dean explains that some authoritarian conservatives *do* change once they become aware of their false beliefs:

> They stop trusting those who are not to be trusted; they put away their prejudice; they drop their mean-spirited, narrow-minded intolerance; and stop trying to bully people. They realize their inconsistencies and contradictory beliefs, and start thinking critically; they learn to deal with the fear that has driven them to find comfort in authority

figures that never really deliver, who would rather keep them fearful.[19]

He does not provide any examples of conservatives who have been saved in this way. Presumably, the occurrence is quite rare. It is comforting to know, however, that at least some conservatives reject their narrow-mindedness and start thinking the way Dean thinks.

The type of reader who finds the above quotation persuasive is probably not "thinking critically." Liberals without logic do not need to think critically, though. They already know what they believe, and they do not need additional logical support.

Conservatives are Mean

The irrational conservatives, according to Dean, are also mean to liberals. He calls conservative celebrity Anne Coulter (the author of bestsellers including *Slander: Liberal Lies About the American Right* and *Godless: The Church of Liberalism*) the "queen of mean," and explains that, "Trashing liberals is nothing short of a cottage industry for conservative authors."[20]

It is unclear whether the author of *Conservatives Without Conscience* and *Worse than Watergate: The Secret*

---

[19] *Id.*, at 183-84.
[20] *Id.*, at 24.

Presidency of George W. Bush believes that trashing conservatives would be a bad thing. Nor does Dean explain whether he intends to develop it into a cottage industry.

Maybe he believes it is acceptable to be mean to people as undesirable as conservatives. After all, they *are* "illogical,"[21] "hostile,"[22] "malicious, mean-spirited, and disrespectful of even the basic codes of civility."[23] Instead of giving them an example of how civil people act, why not be malicious and mean-spirited right back at them?

Here, again, it is difficult to see how conservatives are different from any other political group. Can Dean really believe that conservatives have a monopoly on malice and mean-spiritedness? Is there any evidence that conservatives are any less civil then liberals, libertarians, communists, fascists, or any other group of ideologues? Does he expect us to believe that disrespect and hostility were unknown before conservatives came on the political scene?

Conservatives Without Conscience does not answer any of these questions. It does not attempt to provide information about any other political group. Its overriding message is that modern conservatives are bad,

---

[21] *Id.*, at 27.
[22] *Id.*, at 39.
[23] *Id.*, at 66.

and that message is music to the ears of liberals without
logic.

CHAPTER 8

CHRISTIAN CONSERVATIVES

Conservatives Without Conscience is particularly unhappy with evangelical Christian conservatives. For these people, Dean writes, "faith appears to trump reason."[24] In the evangelicals' defense, however, faith *does* seem to be a central tenet of most religions. One doubts the evangelical Christians would be very religious if reason trumped their faith. Similarly, one suspects that faith may trump reason for many other religious groups, including groups that tend to oppose the conservative movement. But Dean is not interested in criticizing those groups. Unlike those other groups, the evangelical Christians are a core element of the conservative movement.

Dean cites Mark Noll for the assertion that "evangelical religion is offensive" and for the idea that

---

[24] *Id.*, at 28.

"[t]he world has evolved, and... evangelicals, so far, have not."[25] It is unclear what is meant by the term "evolved" in this case. Regardless of its meaning, in a country that respects religious freedom, one would expect the evangelicals to be free to "evolve" or not, according to the dictates of their own consciences. The accusation that evangelical religion is offensive is, itself, offensive. Not surprisingly, it is unsupported by any meaningful evidence.

Dean takes an untenable position regarding respect for religious groups. On the one hand he criticizes Pat Robertson, an evangelical, for allegedly making derogatory statements about Judaism.[26] Although Dean provides little evidence of the alleged derogatory statements, such statements, if made, would be fairly criticized. But on the other hand, Dean himself criticizes evangelical Christians. He apparently feels no need to avoid derogatory statements about *their* religion. Dean acknowledges that it is wrong to appeal to anti-Jewish bias. Why is it acceptable, then, for him to appeal to anti-evangelical-Christian bias? He provides no answer.

One also wonders what other religions are deemed "offensive" by Dean or the sources he cites. How does he

---

[25] *Id.*, at 97, *citing* Ethics & Public Policy Center, "Center Conversations," 18.

[26] John W. Dean, CONSERVATIVES WITHOUT CONSCIENCE (2006), page 106.

feel about Islam? Buddhism? Hinduism? If it is reprehensible for a conservative to criticize a religious group, then surely it is reprehensible for a non-conservative to criticize a religious group. The fact that the group being criticized aligns itself with the conservative movement should make no difference.

In a four-page passage, *Conservatives Without Conscience* accuses J. Edgar Hoover, the former FBI director, of burglary, blackmail, racism, and various other serious improprieties. To Dean, however, those are not his greatest faults:

> Hoover's true legacy,... is more subtle and insidious, for it was he with his fanaticism who planted the seeds from which contemporary social and cultural conservatism has grown. Hoover's focus on the American family and Christianity attracted an earlier generation of adamant anticommunists, who have become today's zealous social conservatives.[27]

In John Dean's view, it is not Hoover's criminal and bigoted behavior that has led America astray. Rather, it is his insidious focus on the American family and Christianity. This insidious focus has, apparently, encouraged various pro-family, Christian types to become involved in politics. This, allegedly, is a bad thing.

---

[27] *Id.*, at 87.

The reader is left to assume that, had Hoover focused on divorce and atheism, the conservative movement would be in much better shape today. Without the fanatical influence of religious types, it would at least be more to Dean's liking.

CHAPTER 9

A DYSFUNCTIONAL FAMILY

Dean calls the conservative movement a "dysfunctional family,"[28] because there are numerous types of conservatives, and they do not all get along with each other. As evidentiary support, he lists ten categories of conservatives: Austriocons, Buchanocons, Neocons, Aquinacons, Radiocons, Sociocons, Theocons, Republicons, Catocons, and Platocons.[29] These divisions seem contrived, but it is undoubtedly true that there are factions within the conservative movement.

It is unclear why this type of "dysfunctionality" is unusual. Any political group of significant size, including the liberal movement, is bound to be somewhat factionalized. A large group, like the conservative movement, is naturally vulnerable to subdivisions.

---

[28] *Id.*, at 19.

[29] *Id.*, at 20-22, *citing* David Wagner, "Who's Who in America's Conservative Revolution?" *Insight* (December 23, 1996), 18.

It is also unclear why Dean thinks a non-monolithic political movement is bad. In a healthy, non-totalitarian organization, members may frequently disagree with one another.

The bulk of *Conservatives Without Conscience* attempts to show that conservatives are authoritarian and tend to support their leaders, no matter how wrong those leaders are. But if that's true, how can conservatives be factionalized into ten different groups? Shouldn't they all fall into line behind one supreme leader? Dean admits that they do not behave in that way when he identifies the factionalization of the Conservative movement.

If Only Conservatives Were More Like Liberals

Even though Dean claims conservatives are factionalized into ten groups and have numerous disagreements among themselves, he frequently generalizes about conservatives as a whole. For example, citing to a study by John T. Jost, Dean laments that conservatives have the following unpleasant psychological traits:

1. Fear,
2. Intolerance of ambiguity,
3. Need for certainty or structure in life,

4.   Overreaction to threats, and

5.   A disposition to dominate others.[30]

On their face, these generalizations seem absurd. Virtually every human expresses each of these traits at one time or another. Who has never felt fearful? Who has not been uncomfortable with ambiguity and uncertainty? Who has never overreacted to a threat? And who has never tried to dominate another human?

Dean answers these questions by explaining that the characteristics listed by Jost "typically cannot be ascribed to liberals."[31] Dean identifies no factual support for this conclusion. He assumes, perhaps, that it will be self-evident to his liberal readers. Self-evident or not, it can easily be examined. Dean's quotation of Jost suggests that each of the following statements must also be correct:

1.   <u>Liberals have no fear</u>. If this statement were true, then one would not expect a liberal to, for example, write a book about how frightening conservatives are. When Dean writes that conservative authoritarians "can be ignored only at our collective peril,"[32] he certainly will

---

[30] John W. Dean, CONSERVATIVES WITHOUT CONSCIENCE (2006), page 30.

[31] *Id.*, at 30.

[32] *Id.*, at 67.

not frighten his liberal readers. Similarly, when he writes that a Constitutional claim made by conservatives "is truly frightening in its implications,"[33] one must assume that he does not use the word "frightening" in its literal sense.

2.   <u>Liberals tolerate ambiguity</u>. One possible example of this tolerance for ambiguity is found on page 135 of *Conservatives Without Conscience*. There, Dean chastises Republicans for introducing partisan redistricting plans, but explicitly condones Democratic plans to do precisely the same thing. Why is redistricting offensive when Republicans do it, but acceptable when Democrats do it? That, apparently, is an ambiguity which conservatives should learn to accept it.

3.   <u>Liberals do not need certainty or structure in life</u>. One is left to assume that it is liberals' indifference toward certainty that enables them to read an entire book about conservatives without ever having a clear idea of what the word "conservative" means.

4.   <u>Liberals do not overreact to threats</u>. Though some may call *Conservatives Without Conscience* reactionary, it is, presumably, not an overreaction. Rather, it is the type of measured and reasonable response to the "authoritarian conservatism" which is consistent with liberal sensibilities. This calm and

---

[33] *Id.*, at 115.

appropriate response is timely, because authoritarian conservatism is at "its highest and most dangerous level in American history"[34] and conservatives without conscience "are capable of plunging this nation into disasters the likes of which we have never known."[35]

    5.   <u>Liberals do not have a disposition to dominate others</u>. That is why, according to Dean, liberal politicians let conservatives make all the important decisions. Dean explains that while Republicans are busy rigging the political system, "Democrats remain silent because they do not want to be seen as whiners,..."[36]

While Dean is willing to closely scrutinize conservatives, he undermines his arguments by giving other political groups a free pass. No rational person can accept the proposition, implicit in Dean's book, that conservatives are singularly evil. Liberals are not perfect, nor are libertarians, communitarians, socialists, communists, or fascists.

Blaming all of America's problems on conservatives is just as fanciful and disingenuous as the scapegoating of the past, which blamed all our problems on particular racial and religious groups.

---

[34] *Id.*, at 117.
[35] *Id.*, at xii.
[36] *Id.*, at 132.

The world is complex. The problems we face, both within and without politics, come from multiple sources. Eliminating one political ideology or preventing one group of people from participating in politics would not lead to a utopian future. To the contrary, the American tradition holds that the more opinions we allow to be expressed, the more likely we will be to find solutions.

Dean has every right to disagree with conservatives. But no rational reader can accept his claim that vices such as "fear" are unique to that group.

CHAPTER 10

CONSCIENCE

Dean boldly declares that conservatives (some of them, at least) are without conscience. For this charge to have any meaning, he must provide a clear definition of "conscience." Fortunately, his attempt to define this word is much more successful than his attempt to define "conservative."

Dean cites to Stanley Milgram for the idea that conscience is an "inner inhibitory system,"[37] and goes on to explain that:

> Conscience checks the unfettered expression of impulses. It is a self-regulating inhibitor that prevents us from taking actions against our own kind.[38]

---

[37] *Id.*, at 42, *citing* Stanley Milgram, OBEDIENCE TO AUTHORITY: AN EXPERIMENTAL VIEW (1969), at 127-34.

[38] John W. Dean, CONSERVATIVES WITHOUT CONSCIENCE (2006), page 42.

When Dean writes that conservatives are without conscience, then, he means that they do not have an inner inhibitory system to prevent them from taking actions against other people. He must mean "bad" actions, because he presumably would not complain if he thought conservatives were unable to restrain themselves from taking good actions.

After introducing the concept of conscience, Dean quotes Stanley Milgram for the insight that "most men, as civilians, will not hurt, maim, or kill others in the normal course of the day."[39] This statement seems obviously true, and is apparently introduced to contrast "most men" to people *without* conscience.

Presumably, then, people without conscience *would*, as civilians, hurt, maim, or kill others in the normal course of the day. It is no wonder that Dean worries about these people. Lacking conscience, it seems, would render a person extremely anti-social and dangerous.

Society could obviously benefit by identifying people without conscience (whether conservative or not) before they go about the normal course of their day, hurting, maiming, and killing.

Unfortunately, Dean informs us, "conscience itself cannot be measured directly."[40] We cannot simply test people for lack of conscience. Rather than take direct

---

[39] *Id.*, at 42.
[40] *Id.*, at 61.

measurements, we must discern whether someone has a conscience by examining circumstantial evidence, such as "stated beliefs and expressed behavior."[41]

It seems as though it would be quite easy to identify those who lack conscience. Because they are unable to prevent themselves from taking actions against others, they must constantly be attacking people. Such expressed behavior as hurting, maiming, or killing should be a clear giveaway.

Conservatives Without Conscience, in fact, identifies numerous people who allegedly lack conscience. Dean never proves that these people hurt, maim, or kill regularly. Instead, he bases his categorizations largely on his own subjective view of whether the individuals in question lack conscience. He does, however, try to bolster his opinions by introducing an authoritarian theory of politics.

---

[41] *Id.*

Part III: Authoritarianism

AUTHORITARIAN THEORY OF POLITICS

The heart of *Conservatives Without Conscience* is its claim that conservatives tend to be authoritarian. Dean tries to establish this allegation with evidence from the social sciences.

He boldly states that, "With science to assist as an analytical tool, the growing authoritarian conservatism can be more deeply probed."[42] This statement implies that there is hard scientific support for Dean's claims about conservatives.

But calling something "science" does not make it scientific. True science requires use of the scientific method, including carefully designed experiments and measurable evidence. Most importantly, true science requires objectivity. Biased "scientists" cannot be

---

[42] John W. Dean, CONSERVATIVES WITHOUT CONSCIENCE (2006), page 72.

permitted to alter results or interpret results incorrectly to agree with their preconceived beliefs. The evidence presented in Dean's book falls far short of being a scientific analysis of authoritarianism.

In discussing authoritarianism, Dean again has trouble with definitions. He explains that he does not use the term "authoritarian" in its typical journalistic sense,[43] but never explains precisely how he *does* use the term.

The closest he comes to defining "authoritarian" is in his explanation of the two types of authoritarians. He creates a dichotomy within authoritarianism by explaining that there are two groups: "authoritarian followers, persons who submit too fast, too long to established authorities,"[44] and "authoritarian leaders, persons who want to be submitted to."[45] Authoritarians then, are blind followers of leaders, leaders who want to be blindly followed, or both.

It is difficult to believe that this type of authoritarianism is unique to conservatives. Lenin and Stalin were not conservatives, but they wanted to be submitted to. The same could be said of Fidel Castro, Franklin D. Roosevelt, and a host of other famous

---

[43] *Id.*, at 45 (footnote).

[44] *Id.*, at 52 (citing unpublished e-mail exchanges with Professor Altemeyer).

[45] *Id.*

communists and liberals. And submissive people have blindly followed each of these leaders.

Dean is not concerned with non-conservative authoritarians, though. *Conservatives Without Conscience* is only interested in analyzing conservatives. In fact, Dean relies almost exclusively on the research of Bob Altemeyer, a professor who has devoted himself to the study of right-wing authoritarianism.

Chapter 12

Altemeyer's Credentials

Because Altemeyer's claims are central to Dean's book, his credibility must be examined. Is he an unbiased scholar capable of conducting an objective study of conservatism, or does he have personal prejudices that might influence his conclusions?

Dean identifies Altemeyer as the author of the following scholarly works:

Right-Wing Authoritarianism (1981);

Enemies of Freedom (1988);

The Authoritarian Specter (1996);

"Why Do Religious Fundamentalists Tend to Be Prejudiced?" (2003); and

"Highly Dominating, Highly Authoritarian Personalities" (2004)

This list of publications speaks volumes about Altemeyer's attitude toward conservatives, and especially religious conservatives. Would the author of works with such argumentative titles be an objective, reliable source for scientific information about conservative authoritarians? Dean answers in the affirmative by referring to Altemeyer constantly throughout his text. Most religious conservatives, however, would probably feel differently about Altemeyer's objectivity.

The liberals without logic reading Dean's book will unthinkingly accept Altemeyer's authority. An unbiased reader, however, must take Altemeyer's statements with a grain of salt. Dean appeals to Altemeyer's authority as a scholar and professor, but even professors can fall prey to personal biases and poor reasoning, and Dean does not provide proof of Altemeyer's political neutrality.

Although a thorough investigation of Altemeyer's scholarly credentials is beyond the scope of this work, there is certainly room to question his methods. The Australian Journal of Psychology published a review of Altemeyer's *Enemies of Freedom* that included the following insights:

> Altemeyer even fails to comprehend what is meant by "Right-wing".... He equates it with the basic lexical definition of "conservatism" -- in summary form "rejection of change". In other words, figures

> like Brezhnev and Li Peng are Rightists and
> Margaret Thatcher is a Leftist!
>
> ...
>
> His alleged scale of Right-wing authoritarianism
> is... an almost complete failure at predicting
> anything Right-wing!... The basis for Altemeyer's
> claim that his work explains Right-wing
> authoritarianism (rather than non-political
> conservatism) is, therefore, a considerable
> mystery.[46]

Altemeyer's conclusions may or may not be scientifically accurate. One thing is certain: *Conservatives Without Conscience* does not effectively establish the legitimacy and reliability of Altemeyer's work. Altemeyer's theory of authoritarianism, as explained by Dean, is inconclusive at best.

---

[46] J.J. Ray, "*Book Review: Enemies of freedom: Understanding Right-wing authoritarianism,*" THE AUSTRALIAN JOURNAL OF PSYCHOLOGY, 1990, pages 87-111.

Chapter 13

Altemeyer's Research

Conservatives Without Conscience presents Altemeyer's Right-Wing Authoritarian Survey,[47] which is the basis for most of Dean's generalizations about right-wing authoritarians. The purpose of the survey is to determine whether individuals are, in fact, right-wing authoritarians.

The survey is provided, presumably, so that readers can test its validity. Unfortunately, Dean explains that he has "agreed not to include the full procedure for scoring."[48] As a result, it is impossible to evaluate the test precisely. Notwithstanding this significant omission, however, a review of the survey's questions gives the reader a good idea of the factors considered by the test.

---

[47] John W. Dean, Conservatives Without Conscience (2006), page 195.

[48] *Id.*, at 195.

71

Many of the questions are designed to single out religious conservatives. For example, questions ask whether atheists are as virtuous as those who attend church, whether there is anything wrong with nudist camps, whether "God's laws about abortion" should be strictly followed, and so forth.[49]

In his text, Dean lists several such questions and states that these "questions would surely be answered in varying affirmatives... by social conservatives, particularly Christian conservatives..."[50] One may wonder what purpose a test serves, if one can predict its results so easily. Dean's statement, however, is probably correct.

If the test is designed to identify Christian conservatives, though, how accurately can it measure authoritarianism? It seems to assume that Christian conservatives are authoritarian.

Altemeyer's survey relies on circular reasoning. The survey is based on the assumption that Christian conservatives are right-wing authoritarians. When Christian conservatives take the test, the results show, not surprisingly, that they *are* right-wing authoritarians. This circular reasoning provides no new information. It teaches us nothing about authoritarianism.

---

[49] *Id.*, at 196.
[50] *Id.*, at 50.

The reader is left to assume that Altemeyer has amassed data about conservatives and authoritarianism to support Dean's views. But this data is not provided for analysis. As discussed above, neither Altemeyer nor Dean have sufficient credibility for readers to accept their claims in the absence of supporting data.

Even if Altemeyer has supporting data, it might not be relevant to U.S. politics. After all, Altemeyer is a professor at the University of Manitoba in Canada. His survey data would presumably be based on the responses of Canadians, rather than U.S. citizens, and Canadian ideological groups do not necessarily correlate perfectly with American groups.

When a study contradicts Dean's beliefs by finding that evangelicals are not uniform in their political thinking, he dismisses the study because its "sample appears unrepresentative."[51] But he sees no need to establish that Altemeyer's sample is representative (if, indeed, Altemeyer bases his conclusions on some type of survey sample).

In summary, Dean does not demonstrate the validity of Altemeyer's Authoritarian Survey and accompanying conclusions. While liberals without logic may not be bothered by the lack of support for Altemeyer's conclusions, other readers *are* bothered. The Survey may

---

[51] *Id.*, at 98, *citing* Christian Smith, CHRISTIAN AMERICA? WHAT EVANGELICALS REALLY WANT (2002), page 3.

succeed at identifying Christian conservatives, but there is not sufficient data to conclude that it successfully identifies authoritarians.

CHAPTER 14

THE "SO WHAT?" TEST

Dean uses Altemeyer's survey to show that right-wing conservatives are authoritarians. For the sake of argument, assume that that conclusion has been proven. We must now evaluate whether it passes the "so what?" test. Why does Altemeyer's conclusion matter? How does this idea that conservatives are authoritarian fit into Dean's book?

Dean makes the Altemeyer survey relevant by boldly stating, on page 61 of his book, that "right-wing authoritarians... can be accurately described as conservatives without conscience."[52]

Altemeyer's research, then, is a crucial link in the argument presented in *Conservatives Without Conscience*: (1) Conservatives are authoritarians, (2) authoritarians

---

[52] John W. Dean, CONSERVATIVES WITHOUT CONSCIENCE (2006), page 61 (citing Professor Altemeyer generally).

lack conscience, and, therefore, (3) conservatives lack conscience.

As the reader will recall from Chapter 10 above, conservatives without conscience do not have inner inhibitory systems to prevent them from taking bad actions against other people. [53] Consequently, they might "hurt, maim, or kill others in the normal course of the day."[54]

So when the Altemeyer survey determines that certain people are Christian conservatives, and are therefore authoritarian, we are left to conclude that such people have no inner inhibitory systems to prevent them from hurting, maiming, or killing others in the normal course of the day. In a predominately Christian conservative area of the country, therefore, one would expect to see widespread hurting, maiming, and killing.

Sensing, perhaps, the absurdity of this conclusion, Dean retracts his statement about right-wing authoritarians being conservatives without conscience. On page 64 of his book, he explains that, "Certainly, not all authoritarian conservatives are without conscience." It is implied that some authoritarian conservatives lack conscience, but Dean provides no test to determine what

---

[53] *Id.*, at 42.

[54] *Id.*, at 42, *citing* Stanley Milgram, OBEDIENCE TO AUTHORITY: AN EXPERIMENTAL VIEW (1969), at 127-34.

percentage of all authoritarian conservatives are, in fact, lacking in conscience.

The reader is left, once again, to wonder how Altemeyer's authoritarianism survey is relevant to Dean's arguments. If not all authoritarians lack conscience, then why does it matter if someone is an authoritarian conservative?

Dean comments that an understanding of authoritarianism "answer[s] questions about why people who call themselves conservatives act or respond as they do."[55] That is a puzzling statement for two reasons: (1) *Conservatives Without Conscience* is not a book about people who call themselves conservatives – it's a book about people *Dean* calls conservative, and (2) Altemeyer's test does not tell us anything about why conservatives act in a certain way – it simply places a label on them.

In the end, Dean's use of the term "authoritarian" is little more than name-calling. The term is always used in a negative sense (authoritarianism is never a good thing in Dean's book), and it is applied, not surprisingly, to people with whom Dean disagrees politically.

For Dean's target audience – the liberals with logic who will accept any criticism of conservatives – the Altemeyer survey is helpful. It gives them the feeling of scientific support for their political biases.

---

[55] John W. Dean, CONSERVATIVES WITHOUT CONSCIENCE (2006), page 180.

But for an objective reader, the Altemeyer survey is a red herring. It is difficult to believe that Altemeyer's research persuaded Dean that conservatives lacked conscience. Prior to Goldwater's death in 1998, Dean had already decided to write a book called *Conservatives Without Conscience*.[56] It was only later, while working on the book, that Dean encountered Altemeyer's work.[57] He then, apparently, used it to bolster conclusions at which he had already arrived. That is not exactly a scientific approach.

In summary, Dean's use of the Altemeyer Survey will be persuasive primarily to individuals predisposed to agree with the thesis of *Conservatives Without Conscience*. Others are likely to find it unconvincing, due to the lack of factual support provided and the ultimate irrelevance of Altemeyer's Survey to Dean's argument.

---

[56] *Id.*, at xxxv.
[57] *Id.*, at 40.

CHAPTER 15

ENEMY LIST

Conservatives Without Conscience is not content to simply criticize the conservative movement. Instead, it identifies individual conservatives by name. The following partial list of people criticized in Dean's book reads like a modern liberal enemies list:

William Bennett. Dean sarcastically calls the former Director of the Office of National Drug Control Policy "Mr. Virtue," referring to Bennett's highly publicized gambling problem.[58] Surely, many non-conservatives have gambling problems of their own. Mr. Bennett's mistake, apparently, is that he has spoken out against other vices in the past.

---

[58] *Id.*, at 26.

Ann Coulter. Her recent book, Dean says, contains "page after page of scorn, criticism, belittlement, and bemoaning of ideas she believes liberal."[59] It does not occur to Dean, apparently, that his own book scorns, criticizes, belittles, and bemoans ideas he believes conservative.

Tom Delay. Dean accuses him of establishing a "dictatorship."[60] Several months prior to the publication of *Conservatives Without Conscience*, Delay was forced to resign from his position as House Majority Leader because of a criminal indictment based on alleged campaign finance law violations. If, as Dean suggests, Delay established a dictatorship, that dictatorship is apparently no longer a threat.

Bill Frist. Dean explains that the potential 2008 presidential candidate "is without question a social dominator,..."[61] But if every ambitious, power-seeking person is a "social dominator," then most politicians must be social dominators. It would be difficult for a socially submissive person to be elected to public office. Dean fails to explain how

[59] *Id.*, at 24.
[60] *Id.*, at 127-28.
[61] *Id.*, at 152.

Frist's dominance is different from that of his liberal antagonists.

Newt Gingrich. Dean reports that the former Speaker of the House "can be a bully, hedonistic, exploitive, manipulative, a cheater, prejudiced toward women, and mean-spirited,..."[62] Assuming for the sake of argument that all those accusations are correct, it is not clear why they matter. Mr. Gingrich stepped down as Speaker in 1999, and is no longer a subversive force in national politics, if he ever was.

Dennis Hastert. As Speaker of the House, Dean says, Hastert "practically write[s] laws [himself]."[63] Dean does not suggest that Hastert literally writes laws himself. He criticizes the Speaker, apparently, for exercising great influence over the House's legislative process. But it is difficult to believe that former Speakers, whether conservative or not, did not exercise such influence.

Orrin Hatch. The prominent senator, Dean says, has been called "a well-known Republican radical."[64] When reading *Conservatives Without Conscience*, it

---

[62] *Id.*, at 120.
[63] *Id.*, at 128.
[64] *Id.*, at 170.

is important to remember that the fact that a person has been *called* radical, mean, evil, or some other negative adjective does not necessarily mean that the person *is* radical, mean, evil, or whatever else.

Tim LaHaye. Dean notes that the best-selling author "entered politics with a vengeance..."[65] as part of the Christian conservative movement. Dean does not clarify, however, why it is inappropriate for a prominent Christian to be politically active. Should access to the political process be limited to non-Christians?

Rush Limbaugh. Dean says the famous radio host "makes his living saying unkind things about those with whom he disagrees,..."[66] Dean seems unaware that he himself is making money by writing unkind things about Rush Limbaugh and others with whom he disagrees.

Grover Norquist. Dean claims the president of Americans for Tax Reform "views politics as war, and invokes chilling language whenever discussing

---

[65] *Id.*, at 97.
[66] *Id.*, at 26.

political matters."[67] Dean provides no examples of Norquist's chilling language.

Pat Robertson. According to Dean, the well-known conservative televangelist has "a history of making anti-Semitic remarks."[68] The remarks cited in Dean's book, however, fall short of what one would normally think of as "anti-Semitic." Robertson does not use slurs or derogatory language. Instead, he makes theological observations that Dean interprets as being disrespectful of Judaism.

Karl Rove. Dean says that President Bush's well-known advisor "has all the credentials of a right-wing authoritarian, and if he has a conscience, it has hardly been in evidence during the five years in which he has been in the public eye."[69] The implication is that Rove's view are not merely different from Dean's, but that they are actually evil. Is it possible, though, that Rove is doing what he sincerely believes to be moral and right, even though Dean would disagree with him? Dean does not address that possibility.

---

[67] *Id.*, at 141.
[68] *Id.*, at 106.
[69] *Id.*, at 174.

Dean states or implies that each of the above individuals is a conservative authoritarian. But how does he know that? Has he given them the Altemeyer test? If he has, he fails to mention that fact in his book. He apparently sees no need to explain any scientific method used to determine that these individuals are conservative authoritarians.

Conservatives Without Conscience labels individuals as "authoritarian" with little or no evidence to support the label. Senators Wayne Allard, Chris Bond, Tom Coburn, Thad Cochran, John Cornyn, James Inhofe, Pat Roberts, Jeff Sessions, and Ted Stevens are labeled as "true authoritarians" because of a single vote they made in the U.S. Senate.[70]

According to Dean, all 122 Congressmen who voted against a particular bill are authoritarian.[71] Even if we assume for argument's sake that the bill in question was pure evil, is it possible that a few of those 122 Representatives are non-authoritarians who made an honest error in judgment when they voted for that bill? Why does Dean jump to the conclusion that all 122 are authoritarians?

As much as Dean criticizes the above-listed individuals, they are not his prime targets. The conservative authoritarians Dean criticizes most harshly

---

[70] *Id.*, at 165 (footnote).
[71] *Id.*, at 166.

are U.S. President George W. Bush and Vice President Dick Cheney. He goes to great lengths to portray them as authoritarians.

CHAPTER 16

BUSH AND CHENEY

Dean states at one point that Bush and Cheney are the supreme examples of "Double High" authoritarians.[72] A Double High authoritarian, we are told, is an authoritarian who scores high as both a leader and a follower.[73] And, as Dean states, Bush and Cheney are not ordinary Double Highs – they are the supreme Double Highs.

At another point, however, Dean states that "[w]hile Bush does not appear to be a Double High, the vice president is a classic Double High,..."[74] With this statement, Dean completely contradicts his earlier statement.

Is Bush the supreme example of a Double High, or is he not a Double High at all? Dean cannot have it both

---

[72] *Id.*, at 183.
[73] *Id.*, at 59.
[74] *Id.*, at 169.

ways. How can Bush serve as the supreme example of a Double High in one argument, but fail to even achieve that rank in another? By now, the reader is well aware that identifying authoritarians is more art than science for Mr. Dean. The occasional complete reversal is, apparently, permitted.

Whether George W. Bush is a Double High authoritarian or not, Dean devotes substantial space to criticism of him. The "evidence" presented against the President consists largely of the rantings of former Vice President Al Gore.[75] Gore complains that Bush reminds him of Richard Nixon because, "Like Bush, Nixon understood the political uses and misuses of fear."[76]

It is difficult to imagine a person more biased against George W. Bush than Al Gore. He lost a bitter presidential race to Bush in 2000 and has repeatedly criticized the sitting President since that time. Despite Gore's historical baggage, Dean does not note any credibility problem on his part.

Dean states on his own authority that, "Nixon, for all his faults, had more of a conscience than Bush and Cheney."[77] Thus, even though Dean admits that

---

[75] *Id.*, at 172-73, 179.

[76] *Id.*, at 173, *citing* Al Gore, speaking at a conference entitled *"Fear: Its Political Uses and Abuses"* (2004).

[77] John W. Dean, CONSERVATIVES WITHOUT CONSCIENCE (2006), page 169.

"conscience itself cannot be measured directly,"[78] he somehow manages to quantify and compare the consciences of Richard Nixon, George W. Bush, and Dick Cheney.

Dean claims, without factual support, that Dick Cheney has created the various "horrible" and "evil" policies of the Bush administration.[79] He explains that:

> Cheney, it appears, knows how to manipulate the president like a puppet, and handles his oversized ego by making him believe ideas or decisions are his own when, in fact, they are Cheney's.[80]

But *why* does it appear so? Dean gives no reasons. He simply states the truth as he sees it.

Dean has proposed an elaborate theory of how decisions are made in the White House today. According to the above quote, Vice President Cheney makes certain decisions and then fools the President into thinking that they are his own. And the President never suspects a thing! Why doesn't President Bush catch on? It's quite simple, really – he has an "oversized ego."

Dean does not reveal the source of his information about White House decision-making processes. It seems unlikely that he is given access to the White House to observe the process first hand. Despite the paucity of

---

[78] *Id.*, at 61.
[79] *Id.*, at 160.
[80] *Id.*, at 169.

evidence, however, he somehow believes he has figured it out.

At times, Dean's reasoning seems overcome by his ideological differences with the President and Vice President. On page 82 of *Conservatives Without Conscience*, Dean claims that many people believe conservatives and Republicans are intentionally adopting policies that would provoke a terrorist response, because they believe they will stay in power as long as there is a threat of terrorism.[81] That argument is more conspiracy than political theory.

Near the end of the book, Dean states, without citing any authority, that Bush and Cheney's activities have been called "radical."[82] Once again, we must note that being *called* radical is not necessarily the same as actually *being* radical. After referring to the alleged radicalism, Dean proceeds to list synonyms for the word "radical," pulled from a dictionary, implying that each synonym from "extremist" to "nihilistic" applies to the President and Vice President.[83] This sort of "analysis" has no evidentiary value. It seems designed purely to appeal to people who are already upset with the President and Vice President.

---

[81] *Id.*, at 82.

[82] *Id.*, at 169.

[83] *Id.*, at 169-70, *citing* Barbara Ann Kipfer, ed., ROGET'S 21ST CENTURY THESAURUS: IN DICTIONARY FORM (1999).

Conservatives Without Conscience has a strong negative tone toward modern conservatives. That negativity reaches its climax when Dean discusses the President and Vice President. Dean's condemnation of America's most famous and powerful politicians is undoubtedly pleasing to his target audience – those we have dubbed "liberals without logic." To the rational reader, however, Dean's criticisms seem to be more a reflection of Dean's own political views than any objective or scientific method.

PROLOGUE

It would be unnecessarily tedious to identify every logical error in *Conservatives Without Conscience*. Dean provides, literally, pages of unsupported generalizations.[84] In this work, I have not even attempted to address Dean's citations to supporting material.

This book has, however, identified the type of appeal presented by *Conservatives Without Conscience*. Dean's book is a bestseller, and has succeeded at attracting a particular type of reader. I have dubbed these readers "Liberals Without Logic."

Before even opening Dean's book, these liberals without logic know what to expect. They expect, and want, a book trashing today's conservative leaders. As they read, they do not question Dean's logic or his

---

[84] *See, e.g.*, John W. Dean, CONSERVATIVES WITHOUT CONSCIENCE (2006), pages 68-69.

factual support. His comments coincide so closely with their beliefs that there is no need for independent inquiry.

Dean criticizes conservatives who present "highly specious arguments that start with the end result they seek and twist the law to fit the conclusion they want to reach."[85]

But with the title *"Conservatives Without Conscience,"* Dean undoubtedly knew how his arguments would end before he sought out supporting data.

Conservatives Without Conscience is not a rigorous study of conservative politics. It is not a scientific analysis of the movement. It is merely a diatribe.

---

[85] *Id.,* at 167.